KOMODO

FUEL THE SUPERNET

2016-2017
A CONCISE KOMODO HISTORY BOOK

Komodo—Fuel the SuperNET

by Christopher P. Thompson

ISBN—13: 978-1981831456
ISBN—10: 1981831452

KOMODO

FUEL THE SUPERNET

2016-2017
A CONCISE KOMODO HISTORY BOOK

CHRISTOPHER P. THOMPSON

CONTENTS

Introduction	....	8-9
What is Komodo?	....	10
Why use Komodo?	....	11
Is Komodo Money?	....	12
Coin Specification	....	13
Milestone Timeline	....	14-15
Blockchain	....	16
Delayed Proof of Work (dPoW)	....	17
Jumblr	....	18
BarterDEX	....	19
Wallet Clients	....	20
Cryptocurrency Exchanges	....	21
Community	....	22
A Concise History of Komodo	....	25
1 Komodo Announcement	....	26-31
2 Komodo ICO Began	....	32-39
3 Komodo Main Net Blockchain Launched	....	40-45
4 Growth and Promotion	....	46-53

INTRODUCTION

Since the inception of Bitcoin in 2008, thousands of cryptocurrencies or decentralised blockchains have been launched. Most ventures into the crypto sphere have not gone to plan as their founders would have hoped. Nevertheless, there are currently hundreds of crypto related projects which are succeeding.

This book covers the history of Komodo, an open-source, publicly distributed cryptocurrency. It was launched on the 13th September 2016 as a testnet blockchain and then, went live, as a main net blockchain on the 31st January 2017. Since that time, there have been challenges which have been overcome by the development team and members of the community. A team of trusted people are responsible for its wellbeing. Major topics covered in this book include:

- Komodo announced on the renowned forum Bitcointalk (SEPTEMBER 2016)

- Initial Coin Offering (ICO) began (OCTOBER 2016)

- Notary node elections took place (JANUARY 2017)

- Main net blockchain went live (JANUARY 2017)

- Distribution of KMD to initial ICO investors commenced (JANUARY 2017)

- Komodo trading initiated on several exchanges (FEBRUARY 2017)

- An attack on the blockchain was mitigated and fixed (MARCH 2017)

- SuperNET attended its first conference in Munich, Germany (APRIL 2017)

- Fiat price of one unit of KMD account surpassed US$1 (JUNE 2017)

- SuperNET Platform formed a partnership with Monaize (JUNE 2017)

- Future objectives of the Komodo Platform put forward (SEPTEMBER 2017)

INTRODUCTION

To be specific, this book covers a concise chronological series of events from the 1st September 2016 to the 1st September 2017. During this time, interest in Komodo has attracted growing interest from inside and outside the cryptocurrency space.

You may have bought this book because Komodo, KMD, is your favourite cryptographic blockchain. Alternatively, you may be keen to find out how it all began. I have presented the information henceforth without going into too much technical discussion about Komodo. If you would like to investigate further, I recommend that you read material currently available online at the official website at https://komodoplatform.com/

If you choose to purchase a certain amount of KMD, please do not buy more than you can afford to lose.

Enjoy the book :D

WHAT IS KOMODO?

Komodo is a cryptocurrency with features including adopted privacy from Zcash and an innovative delayed proof of work (dPoW) consensus mechanism. By utilising dPoW, any compatible blockchain can notarise its hashes to the Komodo blockchain which, in turn, notarises its hashes to the Bitcoin blockchain. This can be considered as two-factor authentication for blockchains or an additional security level. Komodo can help secure other blockchains.

It is also described as BitcoinDark (BTCD) 2.0 (a former coin created by SuperNET). BitcoinDark had its limitations in terms of privacy technology, hence Komodo was created to take advantage of zero knowledge proofs derived from Zcash. Overall, it is a major addition to SuperNET (the parent platform of Komodo). It is an ambitious vision to help solve the myriad of problems encountered in the cryptocurrency space and, ultimately, increase mainstream cryptocurrency adoption.

An ICO (Initial Coin Offering) took place from the 15th October 2016 to the 20th November 2016. Bitcoin raised during this period helped to:

- Fund a larger development team to alleviate the workload being done by lead developer James Lee (user "jl777").

- Fund high capacity notary nodes.

- Fund a faster rate of development than would otherwise had been the case.

Komodo is also:

- Money   —KMD plays a central role as currency in the KMD economy.

- Fuel   —KMD will be required to pay for decentralised applications.

- A Gateway   —KMD will be required to access other decentralised assets.

WHY USE KOMODO?

Like all cryptocurrencies, people have chosen to adopt Komodo as a medium of exchange/storage through personal choice. An innovative feature of the coin, an affinity towards the brand or high confidence in the community could be reasons why they have done so. Key benefits of using Komodo are:

- It is a useful medium of exchange via which value can be transferred internationally for a fraction of the cost of other conventional methods.

- Komodo eliminates the need for a trusted third party such as a bank, clearing house or other centralised authority (e.g. PayPal). All transactions are solely from one person to another (peer-to-peer).

- Komodo has the potential to engage people worldwide who are without a bank account (unbanked).

- Komodo is immune from the effects of hyperinflation, unlike the current fiat monetary systems around the world.

Other reasons officially cited for using Komodo are:

Simple: Komodo Platform will offer help and services to businesses.

Flexible: Developers in business can choose to create their own independent blockchain which is connected to the parent Komodo chain. By doing so, they are not bound or restricted. Instead, they are free to enjoy all the benefits.

Secure: The Komodo blockchain is secure, stable and privacy orientated. The team describe it as offering ultimate peace of mind.

IS KOMODO MONEY?

Money is a form of acceptable, convenient and valued medium of payment for goods and services within an economy. It allows two parties to exchange goods or services without the need to barter. This eradicates the potential situation where one party of the two may not want what the other has to offer. The main properties of money are:

- **As a medium of exchange**—money can be used as a means to buy/sell goods/services without the need to barter.

- **A unit of account**—a common measure of value wherever one is in the world.

- **Portable**—easily transferred from one party to another. The medium used can be easily carried.

- **Durable**—all units of the currency can be lost, but not destroyed.

- **Divisible**—each unit can be subdivided into smaller fractions of that unit.

- **Fungible**— each unit of account is the same as every other unit within the medium (1 KMD = 1 KMD).

- **As a store of value**—it sustains its purchasing power (what it can buy) over long periods of time.

Komodo easily satisfies the first six characteristics. Taking into account the last characteristic, the value of Komodo, like all currencies, comes from people willing to accept it as a medium of exchange for payment of goods or services. Additionally, it must be a secure way to store personal wealth. As it gets adopted by more individuals or merchants, its intrinsic value will increase accordingly.

COIN SPECIFICATION

At the time of publication of this book, its current specification is:

Unit of Account:	KMD
Time of Announcement:	1st September 2016 at 18:59:27 UTC
Time of Original Launch:	31st January 2017
Block Number One Generated:	13th September 2016 at 29:04:01 UTC (testnet)
Founder:	jl777
Lead Developer:	jl777
Hashing Algorithm:	Equihash
Timestamping Algorithm:	Delayed Proof of Work (dPoW)
Initial Number of Coins:	100,000,000 KMD
Total Coins:	200,000,000 KMD (maximum after 14 years)
Block Reward:	3 KMD

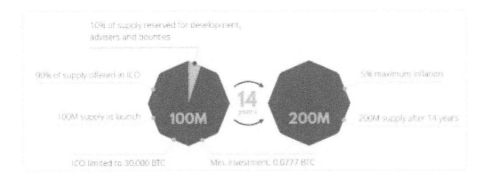

MILESTONE TIMELINE

1st September 2016	—Komodo announced on Bitcointalk at 18:59:27 UTC
13th September 2016	—Blockchain (originally the testnet) launched
13th September 2016	—Official Komodo Facebook page founded
11th October 2016	—Notary node elections website went live
15th October 2016	—KMD ICO began at 15:00 UTC
16th October 2016	—Over 1,000 BTC had been raised via the KMD ICO
23rd October 2016	—Over 2,000 BTC had been raised via the KMD ICO
28th October 2016	—Komodo Platform interviewed by CoinInterview
28th October 2016	—ca333 joined the team as Head of Security
7th November 2016	—2FA became active on the KMD ICO website
20th November 2016	—KMD ICO ended successfully at 15:00 UTC
27th November 2016	—Deadline to become a notary node candidate passed
6th December 2016	—Nazmul Alam announced as part of the team
7th December 2016	—Mihail Fedorov announced as part of the team
8th January 2017	—BTCD deposit feature enabled on KMD ICO website
15th January 2017	—Notary node elections began
15th January 2017	—BTCD snapshot occurred at block number 1,486,000
29th January 2017	—Notary node election results were published
31st January 2017	—Testnet transitioned to the main net blockchain
31st January 2017	—Iguana desktop wallet client was released
31st January 2017	—Distribution of KMD units of account began
1st February 2017	—CoinExchnage.io initiated active KMD trading
2nd February 2017	—Cryptox.pl initiated active KMD trading
3rd February 2017	—Cryptopia initiated active KMD trading

MILESTONE TIMELINE

5th February 2017	—Komodo was added to www.coinmarketcap.com
11th February 2017	—Bittrex initiated active KMD trading
13th March 2017	—An attacker exploited the KMD code (found a bug)
18th March 2017	—Hard fork occurred at block number 241,777
21st March 2017	—Iguana renamed to Agama
6th April 2017	—SuperNET Platform attended BlockShow Europe 2017
17th May 2017	—ShapeShift digital asset exchange added Komodo
19th May 2017	—SuperNET Platform attended a conference in Prague
3rd June 2017	—Price of one unit of KMD account surpassed US$1
3rd June 2017	—KMD Market Capitalisation surpassed US$100 million
16th June 2017	—SuperNET attended the Amsterdam Meetup
18th June 2017	—Price of one unit of KMD account surpassed US$2
26th June 2017	—Money 20/20 FinTech Conference began
28th June 2017	—Money 20/20 FinTech Conference ended
28th June 2017	—SuperNET Platform formed partnership with Monaize
20th July 2017	—SuperNET attended the Barcelona Blockchain Meetup
1st September 2017	—Future objective of the Komodo Platform put forward

BLOCKCHAIN

Every cryptocurrency has a corresponding blockchain within its decentralised network protocol. Komodo is no different in this sense. A blockchain is simply described as a general public ledger of all transactions and blocks ever executed since the very first block. In addition, it continuously updates in real time each time a new block is successfully mined. Blocks enter the blockchain in such a manner that each block contains the hash of the previous one. It is therefore utterly resistant to modification along the chain since each block is related to the prior one. Consequently, the problem of doubling-spending is solved.

Block number one of the Komodo blockchain timestamped at 20:04:01 UTC on the 1st September 2016. It was originally the testnet blockchain, but later became the main net blockchain on the 31st January 2017.

As a means for members of the general public to view the blockchain, web developers have designed and implemented block explorers. They tend to present different layouts, statistics and charts. Some explorers are more extensive in terms of the information given. Usual statistics included are:

- **Height of block**   —the block number of the network.

- **Time of block**   —the time at which the block was timestamped to the blockchain.

- **Transactions**   —the number of transactions in that particular block.

- **Total Sent**   —the total amount of cryptocurrency sent in that particular block.

- **Block Reward**   —how many coins were generated in the block (added to the overall coin circulation).

DELAYED PROOF OF WORK (dPoW)

One of the major innovations of the Komodo Platform; delayed proof of work gives the Komodo blockchain further security. It utilises the hashrate (processing power) of the Bitcoin blockchain which, in turn, is secured via immense hashrate. Elected notary nodes are responsible for creating "custom transactions" on the BTC blockchain. These transactions act as the indestructible record that secures Komodo. On the 29th January 2017, a total of 59 notary nodes were elected from across the globe. Three extra development notary nodes had already been chosen.

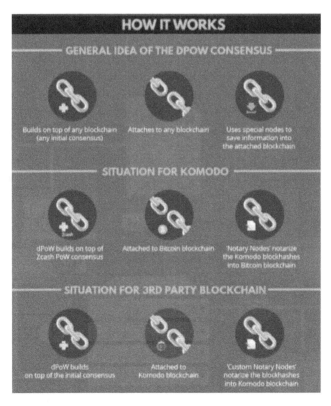

JUMBLR

According to information presented on the website https://jumblr.info, Jumblr was described on the 18th February 2017 as follows:

"**Although Bitcoin provides countless advantages, privacy is not one of them. For a long time, users have had to trust centralized mixers with their coins and pay steep fees in order to protect their privacy with a system that isn't very efficient to begin with. Making changes in Bitcoin itself to accommodate an anonymous factor would also prove to be a challenge as can be seen in the everlasting scaling debate. However, with the launch of Komodo , the first DPoW (Delayed Proof of Work) cryptocurrency with zero knowledge properties, the tools needed to build an efficient and decentralized mixing service for Bitcoin have now become available. This is exactly what the SuperNET team built. This mixer is called Jumblr and it's more like a decentralized anonymizer that can be accessed through the Agama wallet. Jumblr leverages Komodo's anonymous features to provide a service that is much more efficient than its centralized counterparts and does not require the users to trust any entity with their coins. So, how does it work? Jumblr starts by taking your Bitcoins and exchanging them for Komodo through an atomic cross-blockchain swap. Once the BTC has been exchanged for KMD, an anonymous transaction (protected by zero knowledge proofs) is made. This transaction will cut off any links to the BTC that came into Jumblr. Now, KMD is exchanged back into BTC through the same atomic cross-blockchain swap method. This process is automated and doesn't required a third-party entity to hold any funds. Since the process involves BTC being exchanged for KMD, it's impossible to trace where that KMD goes on the Bitcoin blockchain and even if you examine the Komodo blockchain afterwards, anonymous transactions are protected by zk-snarks and cannot be viewed by anyone else. Not only is Jumblr completely untraceable, it is also cheaper. The average fee for a Jumblr transaction is 0.3%, which is only a fraction of what a Bitcoin mixer usually charges. Jumblr is currently being tested. You can participate in testing by joining the SuperNET team and accessing the #Jumblr channel..**"

BARTERDEX

BarterDEX is officially described, in terms of the associated whitepaper, as a decentralised, open source cryptocurrency exchange, powered by atomic swap technology. It is an integral part of the larger open source Komodo Platform.

Cryptocurrency traders are accustomed to buying and selling coins on exchanges which are centralised. There have been many instances of fraud, thefts, successful hacks and other dubious activities of these centralised services. It can also be said that users have to trust such services are being honest and unbiased with their coins. BarterDEX aims to solve these weaknesses by allowing people to trade Komodo, and other assets, with each other without the worry of counterparty risk.

The major aspect of the technology is atomic swaps. An article written by JP Buntinx from https://themerkle.com/ described it as follows:

"It allows users to cross-trade different cryptocurrencies without relying on centralized parties. If user A has bitcoin, and user B wants Ethereum Classic, for example, they can agree to a fixed trading price and complete the transaction immediately."

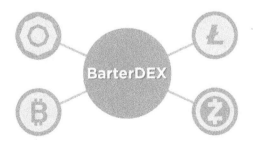

WALLET CLIENTS

A wallet is basically a piece of software that can be used on a personal computer, tablet or smartphone. It allows users to store KMD, and other assets, as well as execute transfers of KMD with other users. Transactions can be either public or private (privacy can be achieved through the use of z-transactions and Jumblr).

Alternatively, it is described as a means to access the coins from the inseparable blockchain (public transaction ledger). The wallet cryptographically generates and holds the public and private keys necessary to make these transactions possible.

At the time of publication of this book, there are different types of wallet recognised on the official Komodo Platform website:

- Agama — an advanced desktop wallet client available on Windows, Mac and Linux. It supports a multitude of coins and has an inbuilt exchange. It also includes Jumblr.

- Komodo CLI — a desktop wallet client available on Windows or Mac.

- Ledger Nano S — a hardware wallet for storing KMD.

- Paper wallet — considered the safest method to store coins offline.

CRYPTOCURRENCY EXCHANGES

A cryptocurrency exchange is a site on which registered users can buy or sell Komodo against other crypto assets. Some exchanges require users to fully register by submitting certain documentation including proof of identity and address. On the other hand, most exchanges only require users to register with a simple username and password with the use of a currently held e-mail address.

As well as being the method by which people can buy or sell KMD units of account, exchanges serve the purpose of setting the value of the coin.

CoinExchange.io was the first exchange to initiate live trading of Komodo on the 1st February 2017. According to www.coinmarketcap.com, over half the overall daily trading volume was occurring on Bittrex throughout November 2017.

DATE KMD TRADING INITIATED	EXCHANGE	KOMODO TRADING STATUS
11th February 2016	Bittrex	ACTIVE
7th November 2017	Binance*	ACTIVE
3rd February 2016	Cryptopia	ACTIVE
2nd February 2016	Cryptox	ACTIVE
1st February 2016	CoinExchange	ACTIVE
17th May 2017	ShapeShift	ACTIVE

Binance is a exchange based in China.

COMMUNITY

A community is a social unit or network that shares common values and goals. It derives from the old French word "comuntee". This, in turn, originates from "communitas" in Latin (communis; things held in common). Komodo has a community consisting of an innumerable number of people who have the coin's wellbeing and future goal at heart. The majority of these people prefer fictitious names with optional avatars. Principal members of the team include:

- Jl777 (founder)   —   Lead Developer

- Ca333   —   General Manager (CTO)

- Satinder Grewal   —   Project Manager / Frontend Developer

- Steve Lee   —   Strategic Marketing Advisor (CMO)

- Audo   —   Content Manager (CCO)

At the time of publication, there are social media sites (and other official websites) on which discussion and development of Komodo take place. These are:

- https://www.facebook.com/KomodoPlatform

- https://twitter.com/komodoplatform

- https://komodo-platform.slack.com/messages

- https://bitcointalk.org/index.php?topic=1605144.0

In essence, the community surrounding and participating in the development of Komodo is the backbone of the coin. Without a following, the prospects of future adoption and utilisation are starkly limited. Komodo belongs to all those who use it, not just to the developers who aid its progression.

A CONCISE HISTORY OF KOMODO

LIST OF CHAPTERS

1 —KOMODO ANNOUNCEMENT
2 —KOMODO ICO BEGAN
3 —KOMODO MAIN NET BLOCKCHAIN LAUNCHED
4 —GROWTH AND PROMOTION

I.   KMD ANNOUNCED ON BITCOINTALK ON THE 1ST SEPTEMBER 2016

II.   TESTNET BLOCKCHAIN WENT LIVE ON THE 13TH SEPTEMBER 2016

III.   KOMODO SIGNATURE CAMPAIGN BEGAN

IV.   PRE-ICO ANGEL INVESTORS SOUGHT AFTER

V.   NOTARY NODE ELECTIONS WEBSITE WENT LIVE

1

KOMODO ANNOUNCEMENT

"A borderless world where horizontal business structure gives a competitive edge. Financial information stays private, and people may save, invest, and prosper without having to worry about politics or corruption. A cloud-based digital economy drives global prosperity." - Komodo Vision

Komodo became known to the wider cryptocurrency community via a forum thread submitted to Bitcointalk at 18:59:27 UTC on the 1st September 2016. It was originally titled "[ANN][KMD][dPoW] Komodo ICO - Zero Knowledge Privacy Secured by Bitcoin". It was submitted by user "jl777" (James Lee) who, as well as being the lead developer of SuperNET, had set the stage to create a better version of a previously launched crypto called BitcoinDark, BTCD. Komodo was going to solve the BitcoinDark vision for financial privacy and allow the team to raise funds via an ICO.

At this point, the team were pleased to report that major obstacles had been overcome during an approximate two year intensive coding phase by user "jl777". Komodo had, until this time, been almost entirely coded by user "jl777". He said there was nothing to bind him to continuing to develop BitcoinDark. Therefore, Komodo had become the long term cryptocurrency of the SuperNET Platform.

As things initially stood, the core team were busy preparing for the upcoming ICO (Initial Coin Offering) scheduled to begin on the 15th October 2016 at 15:00 UTC. They promised to make the process as transparent as possible, so every holder of BTCD would have the opportunity to swap for KMD. Once a snapshot of the BTCD blockchain had taken place, holders would then have one year to swap.

Other details disclosed about the ICO were:

- 90 million KMD will be distributed, in proportions yet to be determined, to those who participate in the ICO with BTC or BTCD.

- 10 million KMD will go towards development, advisers and bounties.

- A fixed initial rate of 0.00532 BTC/BTCD had been calculated by adding 50% to the daily closing price average of August of the BTCD trading markets.

- The BTCD/KMD and BTC/KMD exchange rates depend on how much money is raised, and they can only be calculated after the ICO has ended.

- A maximum 30,000 BTC fund ceiling.

On the 12th September, the team announced available bounties. Only translation bounties and a signature campaign, no social media bounties, went ahead. A bounty was available of 0.1 BTC (paid in KMD after the ICO) each for translating the official Komodo Bitcointalk thread into either Spanish, Chinese, French, German or Portuguese.

The first block of the KMD blockchain timestamped on the 13th September 2016, but it served as the testnet blockchain until the 31st January 2017.

Block #1 (Reward 100,000,000 KMD) September 13th 2016 at 08:04:01 PM UTC

Within twenty four hours, all translation bounties had been reserved.

On the 17th September at 13:17:47 UTC, a separate Bitcointalk forum thread was created especially for the "Komodo Signature and Avatar Campaign". Bitcointalk forum users were given the chance to earn BTC and show support for Komodo by participating. Rewards were based on the status rank of users on the forum:

Bitcointalk Position	Reward for making 25-149 posts during the campaign	Reward for making 150+ posts during the campaign
Member	0.0040 BTC/week	0.0080 BTC/week
Full Member	0.0045 BTC/week	0.0090 BTC/week
Senior Member	0.0050 BTC/week	0.0100 BTC/week
Hero Member	0.0075 BTC/week	0.0150 BTC/week
Legendary Member	0.0075 BTC/week	0.0150 BTC/week

Besides investing in the ICO, the Komodo Platform welcomed "Pre-ICO Angel Investors". On the 9th October 2016, they announced the terms as follows:

- Investments >250 BTC will receive 30% bonus, instead of 25%

- Investments >500 BTC will receive 35% bonus, instead of 25%

- The Offer will end when the ICO begins on the 15th October 2016.

- The total amount that can be raised with these terms is 5,000 BTC.

Potential investors were asked to contact TwinWinNerD to take advantage of the deal. It would be a manual process. By the 11th October, 300 BTC had been raised so far (unknown if it was raised from one investor or multiple investors).

On the 11th October 2016, a website related to the upcoming notary node elections at http://komodoelection.com went live. Anyone interested in becoming a candidate was encouraged to create a profile there. All profiles were manually approved to reduce the risk of spam and accepted within twenty four hours. A screenshot of the election website can be seen immediately below.

Two days before the ICO began, the development of Komodo was well underway. There were some people who were testing the dPoW (delayed proof of work) notarisation on the testnet blockchain and others working on Iguana (the bespoke desktop wallet client which later became known as Agama). Other tasks included a revamp of the official KMD website to contain longer descriptions of core team members. User "jl777" was predominantly responsible for development decisions and the overall roadmap, but not for the KMD ICO Campaign, other KMD related websites or GUIs (Graphical User Interfaces).

Plans were being drawn up to use the ICO funds, once raised, conservatively . An ICO website, accessible via the official website at http://komodoplatform.com, had already been created. A countdown timer was clearly visible to all interested parties. Once it hit zero on the 15th October 2016 at 15:00 UTC, investors could henceforth deposit Bitcoin, BTC, at a minimum of 0.0777 BTC each time.

Followers of Komodo were warmly welcomed to join the official SuperNET Slack Channel at https://komodo-platform.slack.com to join the discussion. There was immense enthusiasm about how much support and recognition Komodo would get.

Other events which occurred during this period included:

- On the 13th September, the official Komodo Facebook page was created at https://www.facebook.com/KomodoPlatform/.

- On the 18th September, the KMD team initiated a competition to randomly select people who had signed up to the official newsletter. One individual would win the first prize of 1,000 KMD, two would win 777 KMD and another twenty five would each receive 100 KMD.

- A 0.25 BTC bounty to establish a Komodo Reddit page was advertised on the 29th September. It was paid after the ICO.

- On the 4th October, another bounty was commissioned for someone willing to be the voice of a couple of Komodo promotional videos.

- On the 5th October, the signature campaign reached the maximum number of 250 participants.

- On the 12th October, a spreadsheet was compiled in order to calculate how many KMD units of account an investor would receive dependent on how many Bitcoins s/he invested. This was regularly updated.

I.   ICO WENT LIVE ON THE 15TH OCTOBER 2016

II.   KOMODO PLATFORM INTERVIEWED BY COININTERVIEW

III. ICO SUCCESSFULLY ENDED ON THE 20TH NOVEMBER 2016

IV.   ICO FUNDS RAISED WERE 2,634.04 BTC

V.   PREPARATIONS WERE BEING MADE TO PUBLICLY RELEASE KOMODO

2

KOMODO ICO BEGAN

"Follow the countdown at komodoplatform.com, at the very second it shows 0 days, 0 hours, 0 minutes, 0 seconds the ICO will begin. Then a link will appear that will take you to the ICO site, where you can register with your email and proceed according to the instructions."

Due to the ICO countdown timer displaying different times depending on which time zones people were located, the team removed it totally and simply stated the ICO launch at 15:00 UTC on the 15th October 2016. It would last 36 days until 15:00 UTC on the 20th November 2016. As evident from the BTC multisig address 35Rwwc9e2Mj7smFXJ1iXF826cMW3tqfz6x, 500 BTC had already been raised from so called "Pre-ICO Angel Investors". There was high anticipation and enthusiasm to see how well the first day would proceed.

On the 15th October at 15:03:45 UTC, the KMD team made the announcement:

"Welcome to Komodo ICO!

The ICO has now officially begun! The link has appeared on the <u>komodoplatform.com</u> website!"

Potential investors were encouraged to register, sign in and participate in the ICO at http://ico.komodoplatform.com. Even though the ICO had begun, development started some time ago. The testnet blockchain launched on the 13th September 2016 and testnet notary nodes were running successfully.

One major use of the ICO funds would be to hire a bigger team. Lead developer "jl777" had been working tirelessly over the last two years with SuperNET and now Komodo. Anyone interested in applying for positions including roles such as project managers, GUI developers, C developers were welcome, with applications sent out at a later date. Above all else, the ICO funds were needed to ensure the full functionality of the dPoW consensus mechanism well into the future.

To be specific, the following table shows the bonus structure of the ICO:

Start Date	End Date	# days	Bonus %
15th October 2016	17th October 2016	2	25
17th October 2016	23rd October 2016	6	20
23rd October 2016	30th October 2016	7	15
30th October 2016	6th November 2016	7	10
6th November 2016	13th November 2016	7	5
13th November 2016	20th November 2016	7	0

Due to technical issues (longer than expected times to log in) with the ICO website, the team decided to extend the 25% bonus for an extra day. All transitions between bonus phases took place at 15:00 UTC.

Registered individuals who logged in to the ICO website were greeted with the following dashboard message

WELCOME TO YOUR DASHBOARD

You can participate in the Komodo ICO quickly and easily on this screen

Your current KMD balance, the current investment bonus, the time remaining until bonus is lowered, and the total investment received (and amount remaining until investment closes) are all automatically updated, and can be accessed here at any time

Generate a Komodo passphrase below and you will then be able to complete a payment to your dedicated Bitcoin deposit address

Within the first twenty four hours, funds raised from the ICO surpassed 1,000 BTC.

On the 23rd October, ICO funds raised surpassed 2,000 BTC. This had, as described by the Komodo Platform, secured a healthy road ahead in terms of development.

On the 28th October at 18:00 UTC, three members of the "not so anonymous" KMD team took part in a live interview. User "coinhustler16" from CoinInterview had contacted them twelve days beforehand. Satinder Grewal (Technical Expert, GUI Developer), Polycryptoblog (Administrative Assistant) and Audo (Community Manager) answered questions and discussed why they introduced Komodo as a fork of Zcash to the crypto world. It lasted 1 hour, 23 minutes and 15 seconds.

Also on the 28th October, the Komodo Platform were pleased to welcome ca333 to the team as Head of Security. He was quoted as saying:

"Few days ago I did a security audit and source-code review for James and the superNET—org and we discussed many topics and potential enhancements in the general field of crypto-security. I proposed a novel solution which we are now working on. I do not want to reveal more than necessary. So far we are the first and only project to use this technic for the usage with cryptocurrencies. It will ease the usage and provide top level security for the average user with no IT-knowledge.—ca333"

On the 8th November, the KMD Platform had the pleasure to point out an article which had been published. Smith & Crown had approached them one week beforehand and interviewed jl777. They described it as true journalism and an in-depth article. The first paragraph of the article was:

"Komodo has <u>two weeks remaining in its ICO</u>. So far, it has raised <u>the equivalent of $1.7 million</u>. This anonymous cryptocurrency has gotten relatively little coverage in the wake of the Zcash launch, Ethereum forks, and recent Bitcoin price activity. This is unfortunate: it has much bigger ambitions than being a Zcash clone. It will be the primary currency of SuperNET."

On the 20th November 2016 at 15:00 UTC, the KMD ICO successfully ended. A grand total of 2,634.04 BTC had been raised to accelerate development. To be more specific, the total number of BTC raised in each bonus period were:

Start Date	End Date	BTC Raised	Bonus %
9th October 2016	15th October 2016	500.00	35
15th October 2016	17th October 2016	980.00	25
17th October 2016	23rd October 2016	606.84	20
23rd October 2016	30th October 2016	286.70	15
30th October 2016	6th November 2016	38.18	10
6th November 2016	13th November 2016	21.34	5
13th November 2016	20th November 2016	200.98	0

Two calculated rates of exchange stated at the time were:

- 1 BTC = 7,747.9 KMD   1 KMD = 0.00012907 BTC

- 1 BTCD = 50.448 KMD   1 KMD = 0.01982239 BTCD

On the 27th November, the deadline to become a notary node candidate passed. A total of 67 candidates had been selected from four geopolitical regions:

- 19 Europe (EU) nodes.

- 20 North America (NA) nodes.

- 13 Asia and Russia (AR) nodes.

- 15 Southern Hemisphere nodes.

Unfortunately, the team had not yet scheduled when the elections would take place. They were also unsure about the date of KMD distribution to ICO investors. A method by which BTCD could be deposited on the ICO website was being devised.

On the following day, a detailed spreadsheet of signature campaign pay outs was published. The total pay out to participants stood at 11.1735 BTC and 16,085 posts were submitted. If participants chose to get paid in KMD, a 25% bonus stood.

During the first week of December 2016, two individuals joined the official KMD team. These were, with the corresponding dates of announcement, Mohammed Nazmul Alam and Mihail "Kolo" Fedorov:

- Mohammed Nazmul Alam joined the team on the 6th December. He joined as a C developer and began working full time for SuperNET.

- Mihail Fedorov joined the team on the 7th December. He joined as a system administrator and developer operations engineer. He had been chosen to run one of three development notary nodes (jl777 would run the other two).

On the 20th December, after innumerable enquires about why the distribution of KMD units of account had not yet begun, the team were happy to clarify the situation. Updates during December had been very slim. They were waiting for updates to the ICO website to end, after which a schedule would be released. The team were sorry for the delays and failure to begin KMD distribution two weeks after the 20th November 2016. A quote from Audo (Community Manager) was:

"We have been successfully testing the BTCD swap feature through an "ugly GUI". The thing works, and now our other dev is implementing it to the actual ICO website with the pretty GUI. We all hope this is done soon, and things will start moving once it is done.

Regarding the wallets: they are being tested by the team. There are still bugs and issues, so they are not published with easy installers. There have been some alpha releases, and multiple screenshots. The team is working hard to get a fully working GUI with "one-click" install ready for the KMD distribution."

Komodo ICO Began

On the 5th January 2017, upgrades to make it possible to deposit BTCD onto the ICO website were complete. If no bugs were identified, the developers promised to activate the swap in the next few days. They were quoted as saying:

"The swap has not yet started. We will send KMD bounties at the same time we distribute the KMD to investors. We will announce the schedule soon. We found (several hours after announcement above) one bug, hopefully we are able to fix it quickly.

Before the KMD distribution we will release the GUI wallet. We will provide some guides / information about how to install it and how to send KMD."

About one dozen questions and answers were published. Some of these were:

Q: Will BTCD get immediately worthless after Komodo (KMD) is launched?
A: No! You can buy, sell (trade on exchanges e.g. Poloniex) and swap BTCD for 1 full year.

Q: I missed the Komodo ICO, can I still invest?
A: Yes, you can buy BTCD and swap them within 1 full year for KMD.

Q: How much BTC were raised during ICO?
A: 2,634.040 BTC

Q: What is the final BTC/BTCD Swap Rate (Base Swap Rate + Extra Bonus)?
A: 0.006511 BTC/BTCD (That's the underlying rate to calculate the BTCD>KMD swap rate)

Q: What is the final BTCD Swap Market Cap?
A: Final BTCD Swap Market Cap = Available BTCD supply * Final Swap Rate
1,289,000 * 0.006511 = 8,392.726 BTC

Q: What is the KMD Market Cap (Total BTC raised + BTCD Swap Market Cap)?
A: 11,616.02 BTC

Q: How many KMD I get for 1 BTCD for how long?
A: 1 BTCD = 50.448 KMD is the official announced BTCD>KMD swap rate! During 1 full year BTCD can be swapped for KMD with that rate (however the exchange rate decreases slightly throughout the year because BTCD staking expands the supply).

Q: What was the KMD price with Bitcoin during the ICO with 0% bonus?
A: 1 BTC = 7,747.9 KMD

Other events which occurred during this period were:

- On the 15th October, the Iguana GUI team released the first Iguana wallet client (version 0.1) for advanced users.

- On the 3rd November, two factor authentication (2FA) became active for anyone wishing to use it on the ICO website.

- Audo was interviewed by Superbcrew. He talked about SuperNET, Komodo and their vision ahead. Details were published on the 23rd November.

- On the 2nd December, Satinder Grewal (GUI Developer) uploaded his first vlog (video blog) to YouTube.

- On the 24th December, Satinder Grewal explained Komodo in his latest vlog at https://www.youtube.com/watch?v=PIRzyjPF5Bs.

- Core Magazine featured Komodo in their December 2016 issue (see below)

KOMODO PLATFORM GATHERS 2636 BITCOIN

The Komodo Initial Coin Offering period ended two days ago. During this 5 week crowdfunding campaign, the Komodo team managed to gather 2636.37 Bitcoin in exchange for KMD tokens. The undeniable success of this ICO reveals, not only an overwhelming need for privacy-driven alternatives within the cryptocurrency space, but also the overall promise that the new delayed Proof of Work protocol and the Komodo Platform offers.

The Komodo Platform offers its users top-notch security features derived from Zcash's Zero Knowledge proofs. These allow users to make private or transparent transactions, according to the requirements of each situation. One of the major differences between Komodo and Zcash are the supply and the way it is issued. While Zcash started from 0 ZEC and will go on to 21 million, until the total supply is mined, Komodo will start with 100 million issued coins that are distributed to the investors. 100 million additional coins will be mined over the course of 14 years. Out of the 200 million coins issued, the Komodo team will keep 5% for development, marketing and bounties, which also differs from the Zcash "Founder's Reward" that will amount to 10% of the Zcash total supply.

One of the most interesting aspects of Komodo is its novel approach on security. Delayed Proof of Work (dPoW) protocol allows Komodo to "recycle" Bitcoin's hashing power by notarizing its blocks on the Bitcoin blockchain. This process is headed by a group of pre selected notary nodes that will be voted on by the community.

Since the beginning of the ICO, the Komodo team has revealed how a series of previously developed projects will form around Komodo to build a complete ecosystem.

The Iguana multi wallet will be the hub where users can access the basic features of Komodo and other cryptocurrencies as well as other advanced tools like EasyDEX. EasyDEX is a decentralized exchange for cryptocurrencies. Using this tool anyone can exchange coins directly and with liquidity. Users will also be able to transfer fiat assets with the same privacy as Komodo, and to exchange them anonymously and in a decentralized setting.

While no exchange has been confirmed, users can count on the EasyDEX decentralized exchange to sell and buy Komodo, once it's finished. Until then, users can learn more by engaging the SuperNET community through the official slack channel.

I.   NOTARY NODE ELECTION RESULTS WERE PUBLISHED

II.   KMD DISTRIBUTION BEGAN ON THE 31ST JANUARY 2017

III.   TESTNET BLOCKCHAIN BECAME THE MAIN NET BLOCKCHAIN

IV.   KOMODO TRADING COMMENCED ON SEVERAL EXCHANGES

V.   AN ATTACK ON THE BLOCKCHAIN WAS MITIGATED AND FIXED

3

KOMODO MAIN NET BLOCKCHAIN LAUNCHED

"We have come a long way, as the development of our overall platform began when SuperNET was founded in 2014. Today we have the core tech ready, and we are preparing for launch"

After weeks of patience from KMD ICO investors, supporters and followers, the launch schedule was published on the 8th January 2017. On this day, the ability to deposit BTCD on to the ICO website became possible. All deposits before the 15th January 2017 automatically granted depositors participation in the future REVS asset token distribution. The full launch schedule published was as follows:

- On the 8th January, the BTCD deposit feature on the ICO website activated.

- On the 13th January, the subsidiary field will lock for election candidates.

- On the 15th January, the snapshot of the BTCD blockchain will occur at a yet unknown block number. The notary node elections will also commence.

- On the 29th January, the notary node elections will finish.

- On the 31st January, the distribution of KMD units of account will begin.

Also on the 8th January 2017, a summary of notary node candidates was posted. It was considered important for members of the KMD community to vote for the most reliable and responsible candidates.

On the 15th January, the BitcoinDark, BTCD, blockchain snapshot took place at block number 1,486,000 at 14:21:13 UTC. This was also the day on which the notary node elections began.

Two weeks later on the 29th January, the results of the election were published. A total of 59 nodes had been elected (16 EU, 16 NA, 13 AR, 14 SH). Adding these to three development nodes, a grand total of 62 nodes were ready.

On the last day of January, the Iguana desktop wallet client was released. It had been tested rigorously, especially in the preceding twenty four hours. It was described as the official and safe release version, but the developers admitted bugs could still be found. As a consequence, they were ready to update it over time.

Original ICO investors were now able to request their KMD units of account from the ICO website. The 31st January is the date on which the testnet blockchain officially transitioned to become the live main net blockchain of Komodo.

On the 1st February, CoinExchange.io became the first cryptocurrency exchange to initiate live trading of Komodo. No official endorsement had been given from the Komodo Platform. They warned the community of the underlying risks of sending KMD to any centralised website, but understood people had to make their own risk assessments and decisions.

An exchange which had endorsement from the team initiated the KMD/BTC trading pair on the 2nd February at 16:00 UTC. It is called Cryptox.

Cryptopia was the third exchange to initiate KMD trading in as many days. To be precise, three trading pairs (KMD/BTC, KMD/LTC and KMD/DOGE) went live. Cryptopia launched on the 6th December 2014. It is described as an incorporated LLC in New Zealand. They aim not to be just another exchange, but to innovate and focus on user experience.

On the 5th February, Komodo was added to a cryptocurrency ranking website called www.coinmarketcap.com. It shows statistics of over 1,000 cryptocurrencies, assets or tokens related to blockchain technology. The initial recorded Komodo market capitalisation on this website was US$11,172,077. Each and every KMD unit of account was initially priced at US$0.111102 or 10,815 Bitcoin Satoshi. What follows are the historically recorded figures derived from www.coinmarketcap.com for the first three days:

Date	Low US$	Open US$	Close US$	High US$	Volume US$	Market Cap US$
5th Feb	0.110987	0.115808	0.110897	0.115808	22,487	---
6th Feb	0.106750	0.111102	0.159718	0.303831	236,727	11,172,100
7th Feb	0.138552	0.160024	0.149072	0.168512	141,788	16,092,200

Over half the total exchange volume was happening on Cryptox in the early stages.

On the 11th February, a United States based exchange called Bittrex initiated the trading pair KMD/BTC. Bittrex began operations on the 13th February 2014 in beta testing mode. Fifteen days later, twelve cryptocurrencies were originally available to trade as Bittrex went live.

On the penultimate day of February, the developers notified the community of an imminent upgrade to the code (master branch). Wallet client users had to update before block number 225,000.

> **Block #225,000 (Reward 3 KMD) March 5th 2017 at 06:25:17 PM UTC**

On the 5th March 2017, the new consensus changes kicked in (see above).

A major event concerning the KMD blockchain occurred on the 13th March. An attacker exploited the KMD code (found a bug) which allowed him to create illicit KMD. It was discovered by a notary node and a fix was put forward as quickly as possible. As a consequence, the developers went ahead with a mandatory rollback of the blockchain to prevent the supply of KMD increasing by ~10%. All exchanges were asked to cease trading activity swiftly. Wallet users, exchanges and other services had to update before a scheduled hard fork at block number 241,777.

Five days later, block number 241,777 timestamped:

> **Block #241,777 (Reward 3 KMD) March 18th 2017 at 03:56:37 AM UTC**

The developers and wider community were pleased the attack had been mitigated and fully fixed. However, the attacker deposited the illicit KMD onto Cryptox and subsequently sold the coins there. A decision was made to refund the buyers with Bitcoin as soon as they contacted the KMD Platform. They wanted to make sure that no person had made a loss because of the attack.

On the 21st March, the desktop wallet client called Iguana renamed to Agama.

Other events which occurred during this period were:

- On the 13th January, the "Bitcoin Rush Show" promoted Komodo.

- On the 10th February, thanks were given to user "roslinpl" for the avatar designs shown at the bottom of the page. Anyone who wanted to promote Komodo, and give it free publicity, was encouraged to display these avatars on whatever forum they wished.

- Also on the 10th February, the results of the "KMD Trading Competition" were unveiled. The competition lasted two days from the 6th February to the 8th February. Users of the exchange Cryptox.pl won prizes based on who attained the highest trading volumes there. First prize was 2,500 KMD (411,224 KMD trade volume) and second prize was 1,250 KMD (365,197 KMD trade volume).

- On the 12th February, the deadline for requesting outstanding bounties earned during the KMD Signature Campaign passed. Only bounties which the KMD team had failed to process properly would be sent from now on.

- On the 2nd March, http://badass.services was first merchant to accept KMD.

- On the 5th March, a new Komodo feature called Jumblr, a decentralised anonymiser for KMD and BTC, launched.

- On the 5th April, it was announced that 32 local currencies, each with their own independent blockchain, had been created.

KOMODO

I.   KOMODO PLATFORM PROMOTED AT BLOCKSHOW EUROPE 2017

II.   SHAPESHIFT INTEGRATED KMD TRADING ON THE 17TH MAY 2017

III.   ONE KMD SURPASSED US$1 ON THE 3RD JUNE 2017

IV.   PARTNERSHIP FORMED WITH E-BANKING PLATFORM MONAIZE

V.   FUTURE OBJECTIVES OF KOMODO PUT FORWARD

4

GROWTH AND PROMOTION

"Indeed, Komodo is a financial platform, and we have a lot to offer. Today's financial world is regulated by the laws and regulations that the jurisdictions around the world enforce, but we are creating a different kind of financial world. We could say that we have a self-regulating financial platform."

Preparations had been made to promote Komodo, and the wider SuperNET Platform, at an event called BlockShow Europe 2017 in Munich, Germany. It was going to be the first conference attended by the team. They had plans to promote Komodo, Agama, Jumblr etc. to an audience of businesses, crypto enthusiasts and entrepreneurs. Two members of the SuperNET Platform called Alice (Event Manager) and ca333 (General Manager) were ready to attend. BlockShow Europe 2017 was being sponsored by Cointelegraph, an online cryptocurrency news website.

BlockShow Europe 2017

Embrace the Blockchain Revolution

April 6, 2017
Munich, Alte Kongresshalle

On the 6th April 2017, BlockShow Europe 2017 was described as a great success. The vision and scope of Komodo had been showcased. It was reported that the team had made exciting new contacts and were keen to attend more conferences. One particular contact made, which later became an ally of SuperNET, was MobileGo. It is referred to as a dedicated token to bring eSports to everyone.

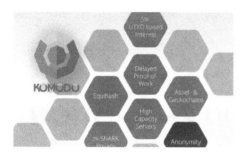 

On the 4th May 2017, the US Dollar fiat price of one unit for Komodo account reached an all time high for the first time since the 6th February 2017. This can be seen from historical data derived from the renowned cryptocurrency ranking website called www.coinmarketcap.com as shown below.

Date	Low US$	Open US$	Close US$	High US$	Volume US$	Market Cap US$
28th April	0.154649	0.163423	0.162859	0.168988	76,688	16,487,300
4th May	0.235905	0.252586	0.304475	0.334389	366,583	25,489,000

It is also evident that the market capitalisation of Komodo had more than doubled since the stated ICO market capitalisation. The chart below shows how the US Dollar price of one KMD unit of account had increased since the 5th February 2017 as well as the sell off which occurred during the attack back on the 13th March.

On the 17th May, a digital asset exchange platform called ShapeShift added Komodo, as well as another cryptocurrency called GameCredits. ShapeShift was founded in 2013 by Erik Voorhees. No account is necessary to swap between cryptocurrencies.

Two days later, the SuperNET Platform attended their second conference in Prague, Czech Republic. It was called the "Blockchain & Bitcoin Conference". It was another opportunity for the team to promote Komodo and their roadmap. Besides Komodo, other services showcased by Alice and ca333 included Agama and Jumblr. Three partnerships were made during the conference in Prague. These were with:

- Loyal   —a modern format of wealth management.

- Vedanova   —develops high-quality web applications and cloud solutions.

- Bitminnix   —a mining company.

Two weeks after the conference in Prague, a major milestone in terms of price occurred. On the 3rd June 2017, the Komodo market capitalisation surpassed US$100,000,000 (see chart below). On the same day, each and every KMD unit of account surpassed US$1. Figures derived from historical data presented on www.coinmarketcap.com for the first three days of June were:

Date	Low US$	Open US$	Close US$	High US$	Volume US$	Market Cap US$
1st June	0.492305	0.501217	0.555246	0.571434	232,006	50,595,600
2nd June	0.530132	0.555521	0.892194	0.935616	1,351,200	56,077,400
3rd June	0.867835	0.934859	1.20	1.45	1,975,440	94,369,800

It was the first time the overall daily trading volume, across all recognised exchanges, had exceeded US$1,000,000 on the 2nd June.

In terms of Bitcoin Satoshi, the values of one unit of KMD account on the 3rd June, according to data derived from www.cryptocompare.com, were as follows:

Exchange	Low	Open	Close	High	Volume (KMD)
Bittrex	35,190	36,000	47,730	58,000	1,786,492.95
Cryptopia	33,540	37,850	40,000	60,000	10,907.13
CryptoX	36,610	36,160	38,530	48,000	1,922.32

Investors and speculators did not have to wait long before the price of KMD doubled to reach US$2. Corresponding market capitalisation and Bitcoin Satoshi figures, according to www.coinmarketcap.com at 1:39 UTC on the 18th June 2017, were US$201,680,043 and 79,980 respectively

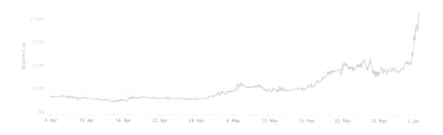

Four members of the Komodo Platform flew to Copenhagen on the 25th June 2017 in order to engage with the biggest players in finance. They attended a FinTech conference called Money 20/20 which lasted three days from the 26th to the 28th June. A large booth had already been reserved (larger than others due to the team having a "two-star sponsor" status). Their booth was designated L12.

It was pointed out that Money 20/20 was the largest conference they had attended so far. Similar to other conferences attended, the team were happy to report that further contacts had been made with a broad spectrum of people, businesses and so forth. One particular partnership formed in Copenhagen was with Monaize, an e-banking platform for small businesses and freelancers. Members of both SuperNET and Monaize met at the end of the conference on the 28th June.

"Both teams see the inefficiency in banking and are actively developing innovations. The potential is endless."

On the penultimate day of June 2017, the first ever Komodo platform presentation, held in Amsterdam on the 16th June, was uploaded to the official SuperNET YouTube Channel. The presentation was part of a SuperNET community meetup which lasted three days. It gave a general overview of Komodo's vision and underlying technology. They welcomed third parties to use their open source ecosystem.

Other events which occurred during the summer included:

- On the 20th July, Audo (Content Manager) presented Komodo to an audience at the "Barcelona Blockchain Meetup" event in Spain.

- Testing of the decentralised exchange called BarterDEX was ongoing. BarterDEX was the main priority over the summer.

- Regular atomic swap tests were being carried out.

One year since the announcement of Komodo on Bitcointalk, there was a lot to celebrate. The team thought that progress had been quiet recently, but were looking forward to a major announcement in a weeks time. They knew the potential of the Komodo Platform, however getting their message out was lacking. A quote from the core team was:

"This transition period will take some time, but our team is working hard preparing to unveil this shining new platform to the world. All our technologies will be neatly consolidated under the Komodo Platform umbrella, including Jumblr and BarterDEX among many others."

Future objectives put forward were:

- To relaunch the official Komodo website at http://komodoplatform.com

- To attend as many conferences as possible all over the world in 2017 and 2018. The next scheduled conference was going to be held in Stockholm, Sweden. After that, they planned to attend one in Barcelona.

- To sustain a strong technical roadmap and solid long term marketing plan.

- To develop and implement Komodo smart contracts. They have a vision to create anonymous smart businesses.

- To collaborate further with contacts made, especially with Monaize.

- To continue atomic swap testing.

www.ingramcontent.com/pod-product-compliance
Lightning Source LLC
LaVergne TN
LVHW052323060326
832902LV00023B/4568